50

COUNTED THREAD
EMBROIDERY
STITCHES

COATS SEWING GROUP

CHARLES SCRIBNER'S SONS

NEW YORK

This comprehensive book of fifty counted embroidery stitches will be useful not only to teachers and students but to all who are interested in embroidery. The stitches have been grouped into families according to their structure, thus making the execution and frequently the final use of each stitch easier to understand.

Counted Thread Embroidery

In contrast to Free Style Embroidery, Counted Thread Embroidery requires no tracing or transfer and is worked by counting the threads of the fabric and working each stitch over an exact number of threads. Evenweave fabric or canvas must be used i.e. there must be the same number of threads to the centimetre on the warp and weft of the fabric or canvas.

Use of Stitches

Counted Thread Embroidery has a number of basic stitches which are generally used. These can be used alone or to create interesting textures as seen in the close-up photographs in this book.

The main groups used are Cross Stitch, Assisi, Spanish Blackwork, Hardanger, Drawn Thread, Drawn Fabric and Canvas Work. Each type of embroidery has a number of basic stitches which are generally used. Other stitches may be introduced to lend variety to a design. Cross Stitch has the same stitch throughout; Assisi Embroidery uses Cross Stitch and Holbein Stitch only; Hardanger Embroidery uses mainly Satin Stitch, with the addition of stitches mentioned in the Hardanger Section; Spanish Blackwork uses Back Stitch, Whipped Back Stitch and Cross Stitch; Drawn Thread and Drawn Fabric Embroidery are developed from the stitches included in these sections.

Drawn Thread Embroidery

This type of embroidery, as its name implies, is carried out by withdrawing threads from the fabric and then embroidering over the edges of the space of the withdrawn threads. Decorative stitches may also be worked over the loose threads which are left when the warp or weft threads are withdrawn. Spider's Web Filling Stitch for example, is useful to fill the open corners where both warp and weft threads are withdrawn.

Drawn Fabric Embroidery

Drawn Fabric Embroidery is created by drawing together into groups certain threads of the fabric. The actual stitching is not the main feature of this embroidery, it is the open pattern formed on the fabric by the pulling together of the threads of the fabric. The stitches are worked over a regular number of threads of fabric and the working thread is always pulled firmly with each needle movement, so that an open work effect is achieved. No threads are withdrawn from the fabric so,

3

although a certain fragile appearance is achieved, the embroidery remains strong and durable. In addition to the stitches mentioned under the 'Drawn Fabric' section, other stitches may also be used to make more decorative designs, some of these are Cable Stitch, Eyelet Hole, Fern Stitch, Back Stitch, Whipped Back Stitch and Satin Stitch.

Hardanger Embroidery

Hardanger Embroidery should always be worked on an even-weave fabric. Satin Stitch is the basic stitch and is worked in groups (blocks) comprised of an uneven number of stitches. When all the Satin Stitch Blocks have been completed, the fabric threads are then cut and withdrawn as required. The loose threads are Overcast or Woven to form bars and various filling stitches worked within the spaces left by the withdrawn threads. Satin Stitch Blocks are worked with Anchor Pearl Cotton No. 5; bars and fillings with Anchor Pearl Cotton No. 8.

Embroidery Materials

The effective combination of fabric, thread, design and stitch, all carefully chosen for their suitability in relation to each other, produce work of real beauty. To achieve this one must use the best materials. The chart on pages 8 and 9 will help you select the correct type and size of needle and thread to be used on a variety of fabrics.

Embroidery Threads

It is essential that the embroidery thread is suitable to the type of fabric used and depends largely on the finished purpose of the embroidery. Whenever possible, it is advisable to purchase sufficient quantity of one shade of thread at the same time, as any slight change in the dye lots might be noticeable in the finished work.

The following list of threads are all suitable for Counted Thread Embroidery although for the worked samples illustrated in this book the predominant threads used are Clark's Anchor Stranded Cotton and Clark's Anchor Pearl Cotton. It is always advisable to work a trial piece before commencing the main piece of embroidery to establish the best thickness or type of thread to use.

Clark's Anchor Stranded Cotton: This thread is a loosely twisted thread with a lustrous mercerised finish. It consists of six strands which can easily be separated and used singly or in groups of two, three or more strands. It is a versatile colour fast thread suitable for most types of embroidery, produced in 8m skeins which are available in white, black and an extensive range of shades.

Clark's Anchor Pearl Cotton No. 5 and No. 8: This thread is suitable for Hardanger and other types of Counted Thread Embroidery, having a lustrous finish with a well-defined twist, which produces a slightly embossed effect on finished work. It is produced in 10g balls in white, black and a range of colours.

Clark's Anchor Coton à Broder: This is a single thread with a highly twisted lustrous finish. Skeins are available in white, black and a range of colours. The dolled skeins can be opened out and easily cut to provide a number of 45cm lengths, which is especially convenient for school use. Coton à Broder is very suitable for Drawn Thread and Drawn Fabric Embroidery.

Clark's Anchor Soft Embroidery: This is a fairly thick, soft thread with a matt finish more suitable for bold effective embroidery. It is available in 9m skeins in white, black and a range of colours.

Coats Anchor Tapisserie Wool: This is a firm, well twisted yarn, moth-resistant, colour fast and washable. There is a wide variety of shades ranging from subtle tones to vivid colours suitable for modern embroidery. Tapisserie Wool is available in 13m 71cm skeins in a wide range of fast-dyed shades.

Needles

In Counted Thread Embroidery, Milward International Range tapestry needles are always used.

Scissors

These should be sharp with pointed blades suitable for snipping the threads and trimming away the surplus fabric in Cut-work.

Thimbles

A thimble is useful for embroidery to protect the middle finger when pushing the needle through the fabric. Buy a good quality one in metal (preferably silver) and make sure that it fits well.

Embroidery Frames

Some embroideries with areas of closely worked stitches are apt to pucker. In this case, an embroidery frame is recommended to help keep the work flat and even. There are several types of frames. An embroidery ring is most commonly used for small pieces of work. The ring usually consists of two wooden or metal rings, fitting closely one within the other, so that the fabric may be stretched tightly. These rings can be obtained in various sizes, the most useful type having a small screw on the larger ring for loosening or tightening it. This allows any thickness of fabric to be used. The section of embroidery to be worked is placed over the smaller of the rings, the other ring being pressed down over the fabric on the smaller ring to hold the work taut. If a screw is attached, this should be tightened. The warp and weft threads of the fabric must be straight in the ring. For large pieces of embroidery, such as pictures or fashion garments (embroidered before cutting the pattern pieces) the work should be mounted on a square or rectangular frame. This means that on completion, the minimum amount of pressing will be required. These frames generally consist of two rollers, each with a piece of tape firmly nailed along its length. One type of frame has slots in the ends of the rollers into which two side laths fit. Each lath has holes at regular intervals at the ends and pegs or screws fit into the holes to keep the frame stretched. There are slight variations to the above description but generally they follow the same method of assembly. The fabric to be worked is stitched to the tape on each roller, the side laths are secured to make the fabric taut and even. The sides of the fabric are securely laced round the laths with cotton thread; if fine fabric is used, stitch tape to the free sides of fabric then lace. Embroidery rings and frames can be supplied with a stand, which leaves both hands free for working.

Your local Needlework Shop will advise you with regard to the most suitable frame for your purpose.

Photographic Illustrations

The illustrations given throughout this book show the finished effect of either the individual stitch or combined with other stitches to creative attractive motifs. Any of the simple motifs may be used to advantage to decorate items of one's own choosing by working directly from the illustration. Evenweave fabric must be used i.e. there must be the same number of threads to the centimetre on the warp and weft of the fabric. It is advisable to check the thread count carefully before commencing as this may alter the finished size of the motif or section given. The more threads there are to the square centimetre the smaller the design will be, similarly the fewer

threads there are to the centimetre the larger the design will be. To determine the size of motifs the procedure is as follows :–
Count the number of horizontal and vertical lines on the photographic illustration and then count the same number of fabric threads vertically and horizontally i.e. on the warp and weft. Mark this area with pins and measure with a centimetre tape. This will give an accurate measurement of the chosen motif or given section and enable the embroiderer to plan the layout of the complete design.

Practical Use of Stitches

The function of the article influences the choice of stitches, threads and colours. If the article should be in practical every-day use, it is advisable to limit the range of stitchery, therefore such stitches as those with 'long arms' should be eliminated in favour of stitches which give a hard wearing texture. A great variety of stitches is not necessary to produce an interesting piece of embroidery, two or three stitches only, used skilfully in attractive colours and threads is all that is required to create an original design. More intricate designs, such as pictures or wall hangings which are purely decorative, lend themselves to experiment with a wider range of stitchery and frequently the design may be highlighted with beads, sequins or metallic threads.

Starting and finishing off threads

To commence or finish threads in embroidery, do not use knots, as they stand out in relief when the work is pressed. Commence an area of embroidery by pushing the needle through the fabric on the right side, about 5cm from the point of working, leaving a short end of thread. When the length of working thread is almost finished, darn in 2cm of the end on the wrong side and cut away surplus; darn in the original end of the wrong side but not where a thread has previously been darned.

Stitch Diagrams

When fabric is correctly stretched on the frame it is impossible to make any stitch in one movement, although for the purpose of the diagrams the stitches are shown in this way with the needle entering into, and emerging from the fabric at the same time.

General Washing Instructions

Use warm water and pure soap flakes. Wash by squeezing gently. Rinse thoroughly in warm water, squeeze by hand and leave until half dry. Iron on reverse side while still damp, using a moderately hot iron. We recommend, however, that designs worked on delicate fabrics or those incorporating beads, pearls or sequins should be dry-cleaned.

Thread, Needle and Fabric Chart

Fabric	Clark's Anchor Embroidery Threads	Strand Thickness
Fine evenweave fabric	Stranded Cotton Pearl Cotton No. 8, 5 Coton à Broder No. 18	1 – 6
Medium weight evenweave fabric, medium mesh canvas, etc.	Stranded Cotton Pearl Cotton No. 8, 5 Coton à Broder No. 18 Tapisserie Wool	3, 4 or 6
Coarse or heavy evenweave fabric, heavy mesh canvas, etc.	Stranded Cotton Pearl Cotton No. 5 Soft Embroidery Tapisserie Wool	4 or 6
Medium weight square weave canvas	Stranded Cotton Pearl Cotton No. 5 Soft Embroidery Tapisserie Wool	3, 4 or 6
Heavy square weave canvas	Stranded Cotton Soft Embroidery Tapisserie Wool	6

Milward International Range Needle Sizes	Remarks
Tapestry Needles (rounded points)	These threads and needles are used for working over counted threads of fabric or canvas.

No	Thickness
24	{ 1 and 2 strands 3 strands, Coton à Broder No. 18 4 strands, Pearl Cotton No. 8
20	6 strands, Pearl Cotton No. 5
18	Soft Embroidery, Tapisserie Wool

Tapestry Needles (rounded points)	These threads and needles are used for working over counted threads of fabric or canvas.

No	Thickness
20	6 strands, Pearl Cotton No. 5
18	Soft Embroidery, Tapisserie Wool

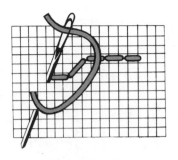

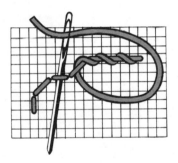

Bring the thread out at the right hand side of fabric. Take a backward stitch over 2 threads of fabric (or the required number), bringing the needle out 2 threads in front of the place where the thread first emerged. Continue in this way, working from right to left in required direction. To whip Back Stitch, with another thread in the needle, whip over each Back Stitch without piercing the fabric. This stitch is generally used in Spanish Blackwork to emphasise an outline.

Holbein Stitch or Double Running Stitch

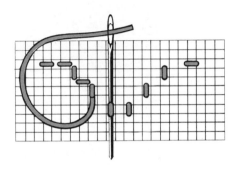

Working from right to left, work a row of Running Stitches by passing the needle over and under 2 threads of fabric (or the required number), following the shape of the design. Work a second row of Running Stitches in the same way working from left to right, filling in the spaces left in the first row. This stitch is used in Assisi Embroidery to outline the Cross Stitch, but may also be used in other types of embroidery on evenweave fabric.

Cross Stitch

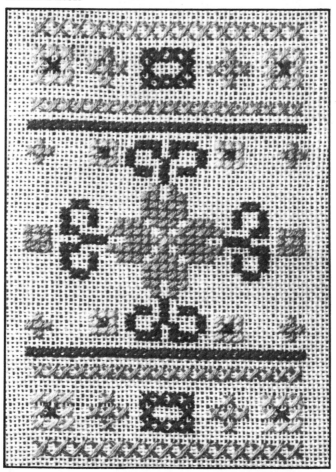

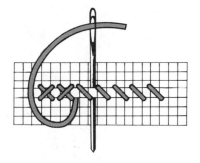

Bring the thread through at the lower right hand side, insert the needle 2 threads up (or the required number) and 2 threads to the left and bring out 2 threads down, thus forming a half cross, continue in this way to the end of the row. Complete the upper half of the cross as shown. Cross Stitch may be worked either from right to left or left to right but it is important that the upper half of all crosses should lie in the same direction.

Double Cross Stitch

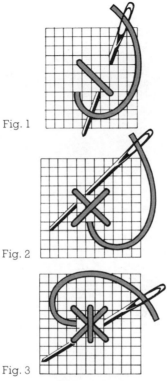

Fig. 1

Fig. 2

Fig. 3

This stitch forms a square over 4 horizontal and 4 vertical (or any even number) threads of fabric. Fig. 1 – work a Cross Stitch as shown; then bring the needle through 4 threads down and 2 threads to the left. Fig. 2 – insert the needle 4 threads up and bring through 2 threads to the left and 2 threads down. Fig. 3 – insert the needle 4 threads to the right and bring through 2 threads down and 4 threads to the left in readiness to commence the next stitch. For the overall effect it is important when working an area of Double Cross Stitch that the last upper stitch of each should lie in the same direction.

Rice Stitch

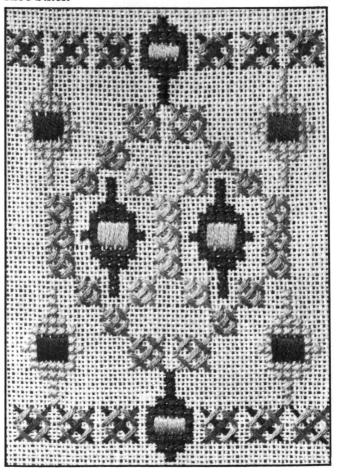

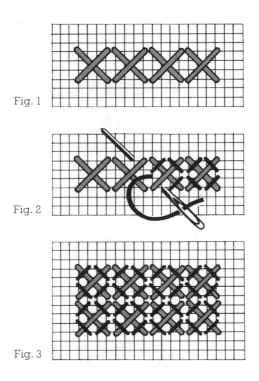

Fig. 1

Fig. 2

Fig. 3

This stitch is usually worked in a slightly thicker thread for the large Cross Stitch and a finer thread for the small Back Stitch. Fig. 1 – first, cover the required area with Cross Stitch worked over 4 (or any even number) threads each way of fabric. Fig. 2 – over the corners of each Cross Stitch work small diagonal Back Stitches at right angles over 2 threads each way of the fabric, so that these small stitches also form a cross. The small stitches have been shown in black in order to show the construction. Fig. 3 – shows the finished overall effect.

Herringbone Stitch

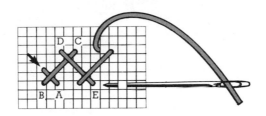

This stitch is worked from left to right. Bring the thread out at the arrow. Insert the needle at A (2 threads down and 2 threads to the right) and bring out at B (2 threads to the left), insert at C (4 threads up and 4 threads to the right) and bring out at D (2 threads to the left), insert at E (4 threads down and 4 threads to the right). Repeat from B to end of row. Herringbone Stitch may be worked evenly over any number of fabric threads and as can be seen in the photograph, it also makes an attractive stitch in Drawn Thread embroidery.

Chevron Stitch

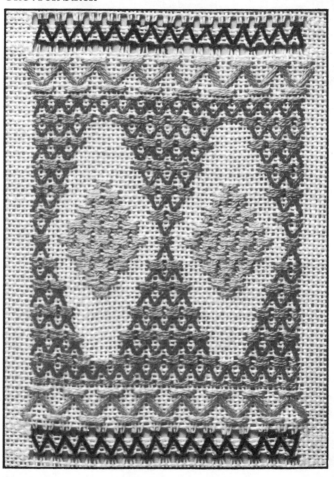

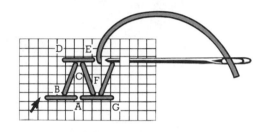

This stitch is worked from left to right. Bring the thread out at the arrow. Insert the needle at A (4 threads to the right) and bring out at B (2 threads to the left), insert at C (4 threads up and 2 threads to the right) and bring out at D (2 threads to the left), insert at E (2 threads to the right) and bring out at C (2 threads to the left), insert at F (4 threads down and 2 threads to the right) and bring through at A (2 threads to the left), insert at G (4 threads to the right) and bring through at F (2 threads to the left). Repeat from B to end of row. Chevron Stitch may be worked evenly over any number of fabric threads and, as can be seen in the photograph, it also makes an attractive stitch in Drawn Thread embroidery.

Cretan Stitch

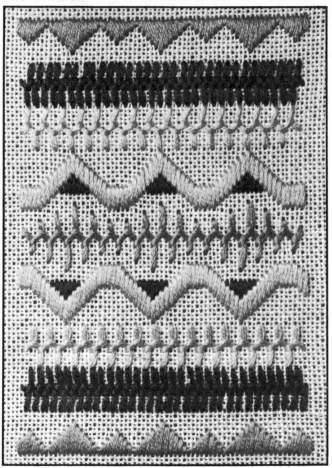

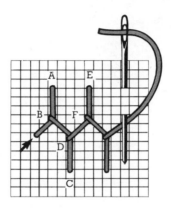

This stitch is worked from left to right. Bring the thread out at the arrow. Insert the needle at A (6 threads up and 2 threads to the right) and bring out at B (4 threads down), insert at C (6 threads down and 2 threads to the right) and bring out at D (4 threads up), insert at E (6 threads up and 2 threads to the right) and bring out at F. Repeat from B to end of row. Cretan Stitch may be worked evenly over any number of fabric threads to form a close or open pattern.

Fly Stitch

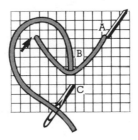

Bring the thread out at the arrow, hold the thread down with the left thumb and insert the needle 8 threads to the right at A and bring out at B (4 threads down and 4 threads to the left), insert at C (2 threads down) tying down the previous surface stitch midway. Bring the needle through at A in readiness for the next stitch. Fly Stitch may be worked over any number of fabric threads.

Fern Stitch

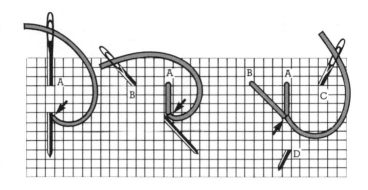

This stitch consists of 3 Straight Stitches radiating from the same central point. Bring the thread out at the arrow. Insert the needle at A (4 threads up) and bring out again at arrow, insert at B (4 threads up and 4 threads to the left) and bring out again at arrow, insert at C (4 threads up and 4 threads to the right) and bring out at D (8 threads down and 4 to the left) in readiness for the next stitch. Fern Stitch may be worked over any number of fabric threads horizontally, vertically or obliquely as shown in the photograph.

Star Stitch

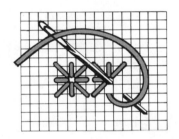

This stitch forms a square over 4 horizontal and 4 vertical (or any even number) threads of fabric. It consists of eight Straight Stitches worked over 2 fabric threads, each worked from the outer edge into the same central hole as shown in the diagram and worked individually or in horizontal or vertical rows.

31

Satin Stitch

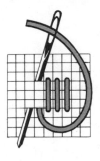

This stitch may be worked from right to left or left to right. The number of threads over which the stitches are worked may vary, depending upon the effect desired.

Florentine Stitch

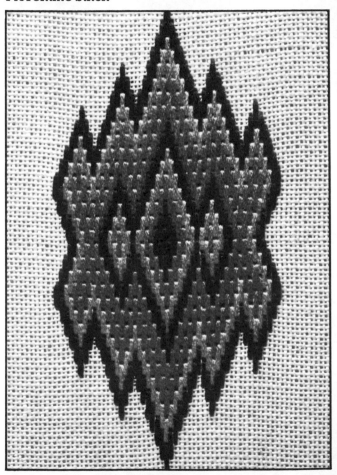

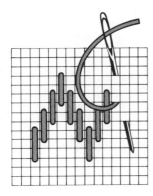

Fig. 1

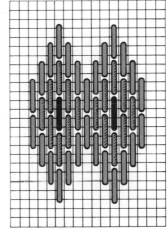

Fig. 2

This stitch is used for working zig-zag patterns known as
Florentine work. It is generally used to fill a large area and is
then worked in two or more rows of different colours forming
an all over wave pattern. The size of the wave may be varied,
depending upon the number of stitches or the number of
threads over which the stitches are worked. Fig 1 – shows the
method of working a single row of stitches. Fig. 2 – shows the
finished effect when using three colours.

Cable Stitch

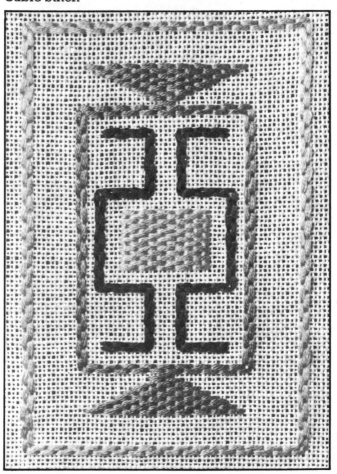

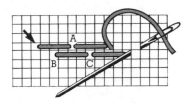

This stitch is worked from left to right. Bring the thread out at the arrow. Insert the needle at A (4 threads to the right, or the required number) and bring out at B (1 thread down and 2 threads to the left), insert at C (4 threads to the right) and bring out again at A (1 thread up and 2 threads to the left). Continue working in the same way to the end of the row. Cable Stitch may be worked evenly over any number of fabric threads horizontally, vertically or obliquely.

Eyelet Hole

An Eyelet is worked over a square of fabric threads of even number each way of the fabric, and one stitch is worked between each of the fabric threads in the square and all stitches into the same central hole.

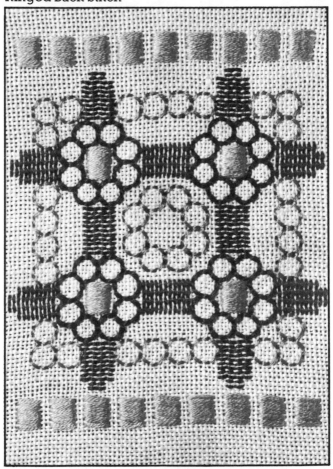

40

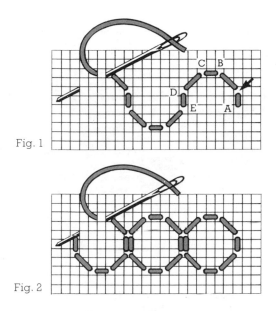

Fig. 1

Fig. 2

This stitch is worked from right to left and may be used as a border or as a filling. Fig. 1 – bring the thread out at the arrow. Insert the needle at A (2 threads down, or the required number) and bring out at B (4 threads up and 2 to the left), insert at the arrow and bring out at C (2 threads up and 4 threads to the left), insert again at B and bring out at D (2 threads down and 4 threads to the left), insert again at C and bring out at E (4 threads down and 2 threads to the left). Continue making half rings of Back Stitch for the required length. Fig. 2 – turn the fabric round for the second and following rows (if used as a Filling Stitch) and work in the same way to complete the rings. The connecting stitches between rings are worked into the same holes. This stitch may also be worked double, giving a bolder appearance. Work as described above but work two Back Stitches into each position. All stitches must be pulled firmly.

Four-sided Stitch and Filling

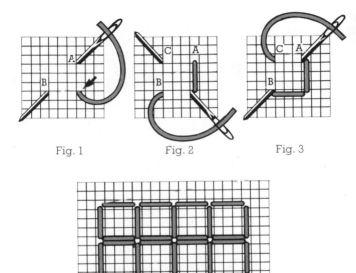

Fig. 1   Fig. 2   Fig. 3

Fig. 4

This stitch is worked from right to left and may be used as a border or as a filling. Fig. 1 – bring the thread out at the arrow. Insert the needle at A (4 threads up, or the required number) and bring out at B (4 threads down and 4 threads to the left). Fig. 2 – insert at the arrow, bring out at C (4 threads up and 4 threads to the left). Fig. 3 – insert again at A and bring out again at B. Continue in this way to the end of the row or close the end with a Straight Stitch from B to C for a single Four-sided Stitch. Fig. 4 – if used as a Filling, turn the fabric round for the next and following rows and work in the same way. All stitches must be pulled firmly.

Three-sided Stitch

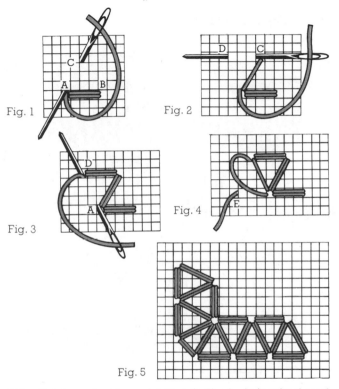

Fig. 1

Fig. 2

Fig. 3

Fig. 4

Fig. 5

This stitch is worked from right to left. Fig. 1 – bring the thread out at A and work two stitches from A to B over 4 threads (or the required number) and bring out again at A and work two stitches from A to C (4 threads up and 2 threads to the right). Fig. 2 – bring the thread out at D (4 threads to the left), work two stitches from D to C then bring the thread out again at D. Fig. 3 – work two stitches from D to A. Fig. 4 – bring the thread through at E (4 threads to the left). Continue working in the same way to the end of the row. Fig. 5 – shows a corner turning. All stitches must be pulled firmly.

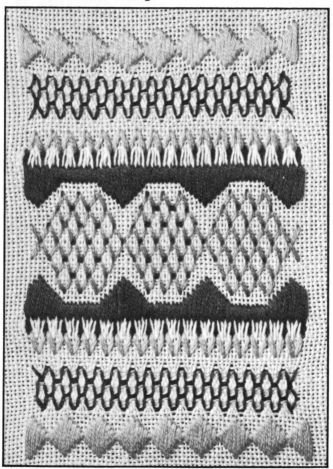

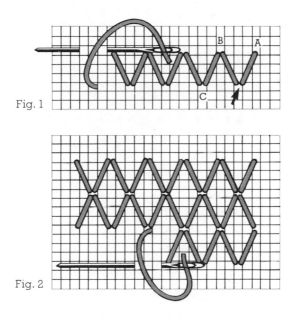

Fig. 1

Fig. 2

This stitch is worked from right to left, it may be used as a simple border or as a filling. Fig. 1 – bring the thread out at the arrow, insert the needle at A (4 threads up and 2 threads to the right, or the required number) and bring through at B (4 threads to the left), insert at arrow and bring through at C (4 threads to the left). Continue in this way to the end of the row. Fig. 2 – turn the fabric round before commencing second and following rows and work in the same way into the same holes in each preceding row to form diamond shapes. All stitches must be pulled firmly.

47

Four-sided Wave Stitch

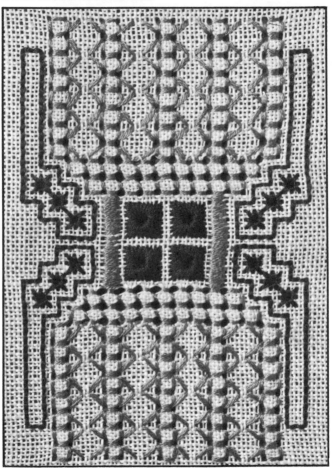

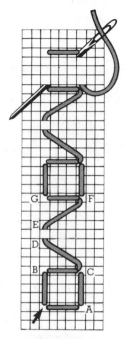

This stitch may be used as a simple border or as a filling. The easiest method is to work vertically commencing at the bottom and working upwards. Bring the thread out at the arrow, insert the needle at A (4 threads to the right, or the appropriate number and bring through at B (4 threads up and 4 threads to the left), insert at C (4 threads to the right) and bring out again at A, insert again at C and bring out again at the arrow, insert at B and bring out again at C, insert the needle at D (3 threads up and 4 threads to the left) and bring out at E (2 threads up), insert at F (3 threads up and 4 threads to the right) and bring through at G (4 threads to the left). Continue working in sequence for the required length, turn fabric, secure thread on wrong side and work the next and each following row in the same way. All stitches must be pulled firmly.

Honeycomb Filling Stitch

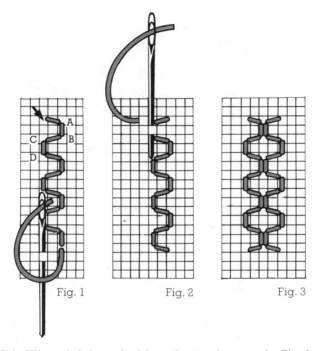

Fig. 1   Fig. 2   Fig. 3

This filling stitch is worked from the top downwards. Fig. 1 –
bring the thread out at the arrow. Insert the needle at A (2
threads to the right, or the required number) and bring out at
B (2 threads down), insert again at A and bring out at B, insert at
C (2 threads to the left) and bring out at D (2 threads down),
insert again at C and bring out at D. Continue in this way for
the required length. Turn the fabric round for the next and
each following row and work in the same way. Fig. 2 – shows
the work turned ready for second row. Fig. 3 – shows two
rows of stitching and how they form a filling. All stitches must
be pulled firmly.

Punch Stitch

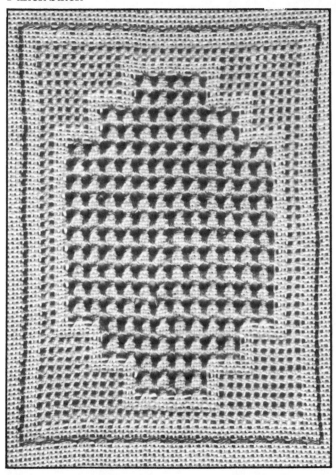

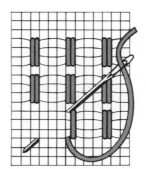

Fig. 1

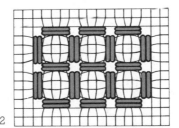

Fig. 2

Fig. 1 – work two Straight Stitches into the same place over 4 horizontal threads (or the required number), then bring the thread out 4 threads down and 4 threads to the left in readiness for the next stitch. Work along the row for the required length. Turn the fabric round for the next and each following row and work in the same way. Fig. 2 – shows the squares completed by turning the fabric sideways and working in the same way. All stitches must be pulled firmly.

Coil Filling Stitch

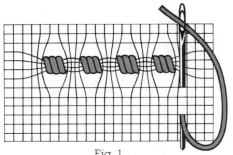

Fig. 1

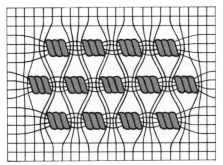

Fig. 2

This filling stitch is worked from right to left. Three Satin Stitches are worked over 4 horizontal threads and between 2 vertical threads (or the required even number) leaving 4 threads between each coil. Make a small stitch on the wrong side into the last group of stitches to secure the thread before commencing the next row. Fig. 1 – shows the first row worked and the fabric turned round with the needle in position for the next row. Continue working in this way until the shape is filled. Fig. 2 – shows three rows of stitching worked and illustrates the alternating position of the coils in each row. All stitches must be pulled firmly.

Linked Four-sided Filling Stitch

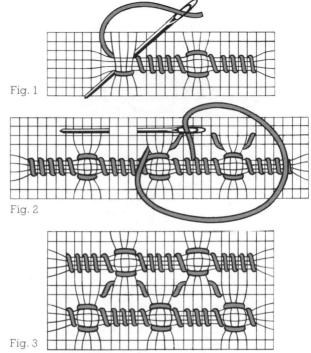

Fig. 1

Fig. 2

Fig. 3

This filling stitch consists of two rows of stitchery worked from right to left alternately. Fig. 1 – shows the first row consisting of Satin Stitch and Four-sided Stitch worked alternately over 4 (or the required even number) threads each way of the fabric. Continue in this way for the required length then turn the fabric round before commencing the second row. Fig. 2 – shows the second row which consists of undulating running stitch worked evenly behind 4 vertical fabric threads and over 2 horizontal threads coinciding with the grouping in the previous row and working into the same holes. Turn fabric round for the next and following rows until the shape is filled. Fig. 3 – shows three rows of stitchery showing the alternate positioning of the stitches. All stitches must be pulled firmly.

Double Faggot Filling Stitch

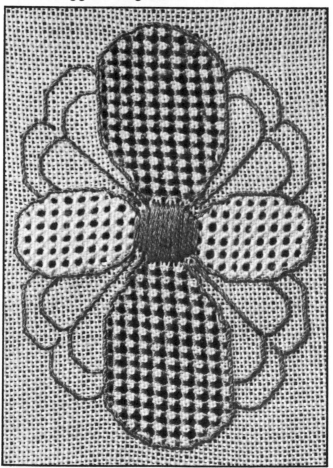

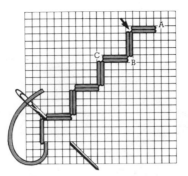

Fig. 1

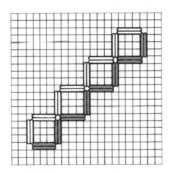

Fig. 2

This filling stitch is worked diagonally in rows from upper right to lower left each stitch worked twice into the same place. Fig. 1 – bring the thread out at the arrow. Insert the needle at A (4 threads to the right, or the required number) and bring out at B (4 threads down and 4 threads to the left), insert again at the arrow and bring out at C (4 threads down and 4 threads to the left). Continue in this way for the required length. Turn the fabric round for the next and each following row and work in the same way. Fig. 2 – shows the second row (blue) in relation to the first row. All stitches must be pulled firmly.

Reversed Faggot Filling Stitch

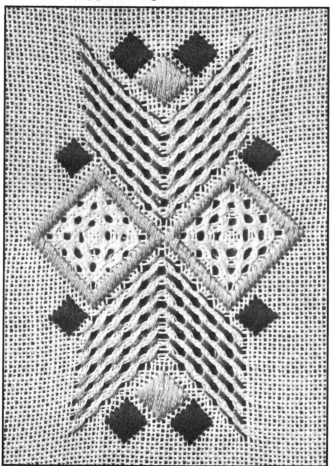

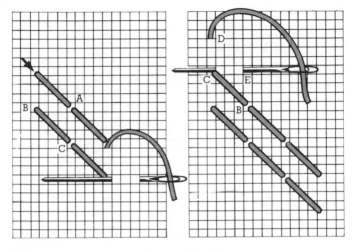

Fig. 1   Fig. 2

This filling stitch is worked diagonally in rows from upper left
to lower right. Fig. 1 – bring the thread out at the arrow.
Insert the needle at A (4 threads down, or the required
number and 4 threads to the right) and bring out at B (4 threads
to the left), insert at C (4 threads down and 4 threads to the
right) and bring out at A (4 threads up). Continue in this way for
the required length. When the needle is inserted at C to complete the last stitch on the lower line, turn the fabric round for
the next row. Fig. 2 – bring the thread out at D (4 threads up),
insert at E (4 threads down and 4 threads to the right) and bring
out at C, insert at B and bring out at E. Continue in this way to
the end of the row. Turn the fabric round and work figs. 1 and
2 alternately until the shape is filled. All stitches must be pulled
firmly.

Diagonal Raised Band

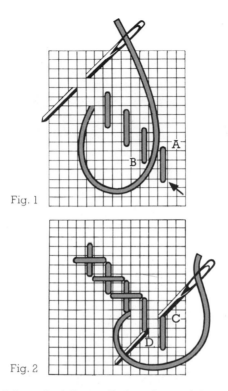

Fig. 1

Fig. 2

This stitch is worked diagonally from lower right to upper left.
Fig. 1 – bring the thread out at the arrow. Insert the needle at
A (4 threads up, or the required number) and bring out at
B (2 threads down and 2 threads to the left). Continue in this
way to the end of the row. Fig. 2 – after completing the last
stitch, bring the needle through as if to commence a further
stitch. Insert the needle at C (4 threads to the right) and bring it
through at D (2 threads down and 2 threads to the left). Continue
in this way to the end of the row. All stitches must be pulled
firmly.

Mosaic Filling Stitch

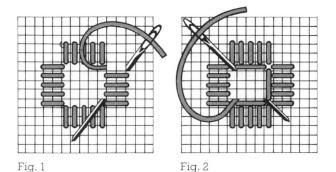

Fig. 1   Fig. 2

Fig. 3

Fig. 1 – work four blocks of Satin Stitch to form a square, with
an equal number of stitches in each block and worked over an
equal number of threads. Bring the thread from the last stitch
through to the right hand corner of the inner square. Fig. 2 –
work a Four-sided Stitch within the Satin Stitch blocks, bringing
the thread out at the starting point. Fig. 3 – work a Cross
Stitch in the centre.

Squared Edging Stitch

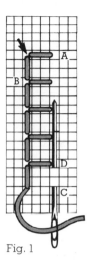

Fig. 1

This edging stitch consists of two rows of stitchery worked from the top downwards. The first row is worked before turning the fabric to form a hem. Fig. 1 – bring the thread out at the arrow. Insert the needle at A (3 threads to the right, or the required number) and bring through at B (3 threads down and 3 threads to the left), insert at arrow and bring through again at B in readiness for the next stitch. Continue in this way for the required length. To turn the corner insert the needle at C as shown and bring out at D (3 threads up), insert again at C and bring out 3 threads to the right at E (see fig. 2). Insert again at C and bring out again at E in readiness for the next stitch. Turn fabric and continue working in the same way for the remaining three sides and corners. Fold surplus fabric to the wrong side, so that the outer vertical stitch stands out. In order to hold the two layers of fabric in position the second row of stitching is shown in fig. 2.

(continued overleaf)

Squared Edging Stitch (continued)

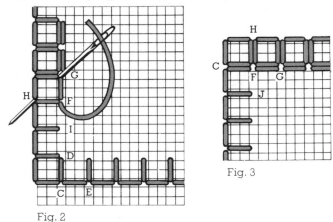

Fig. 2

Fig. 3

Fig. 2 – commence at least 4 vertical stitches down from a corner. Insert the needle from the wrong side through two layers of fabric (3 threads to the right of the outer vertical stitch) and bring through at F, insert at G (3 threads up), bring out again at F and insert again at G; pass the thread diagonally behind the work and bring round at H, insert again at F and bring through at I in readiness for the next stitch. Continue in this way to within 4 vertical stitches from corner. Before bringing the thread round at H, fold back the fabric to form the corner (4 layers of fabric), insert the needle through the third and fourth layers of fabric and bring through 3 threads from folded edge on wrong side and pass the thread diagonally behind the work and bring round at H; continue working in this way to the corner. Fig. 3 – turn the fabric as shown and bring needle through at F, insert at G, bring through again at F, insert again at G and bring round at H, insert again at F and bring round at C, insert again at F and bring out at J in readiness for the next stitch. Continue as in fig. 2. Work round article in this way until complete. Trim away surplus fabric on wrong side, close to the double line of stitching. All stitches must be pulled firmly.

Pointed Edging Stitch
Working diagrams on following pages.

Pointed Edging Stitch (continued)

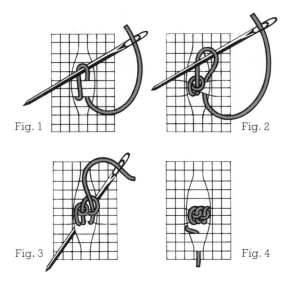

Fig. 1

Fig. 2

Fig. 3

Fig. 4

This edging stitch consists of two rows of stitchery worked from the top downwards. The first row Hedebo Buttonhole Stitch is worked before turning the fabric to form a hem. Fig. 1 – shows the method of working one Hedebo Buttonhole Stitch over 3 horizontal fabric threads (or the required number) and between 2 vertical fabric threads. Fig. 2 – shows the second stitch worked into the same place, the working thread is pulled firmly in each stitch to form a knot. Fig. 3 – shows the completion of the second stitch and the needle passing behind the fabric and knot just made and emerging 3 threads down and 1 thread to the left, this movement anchors the two stitches just made. Fig. 3 – shows the working thread passed over 1 thread to the right and coming out 3 threads down between the same pair of vertical fabric threads in readiness for the next stitch.

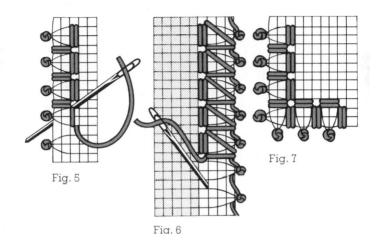

Fig. 5

Fig. 6

Fig. 7

Continue in this way until the required number of knots and corners have been worked. Fold fabric to wrong side, so that the Hedebo Buttonhole Stitch stands out like small knots, the fabric is then held in position by working the second row of stitching, Open-sided Square Stitch. Each stitch is worked twice into the same place as shown in fig. 5. *NOTE – The needle is inserted 4 threads from the knot on the wrong side and pulled through 3 threads from the knot on the right side (see figs. 5 and 6).* Work Open-sided Square Stitch to within four knots from corner, trim away surplus fabric close to the stitching on the completed side, fold back fabric on second side in the same way as before and trim so that it does not extend beyond the fourth knot when folded, continue working the Open-sided Square Stitch. Fig. 6 – shows the reverse side of fabric. Fig. 7 – shows a corner turning, right side of fabric. All stitches must be pulled firmly.

Pin Stitch

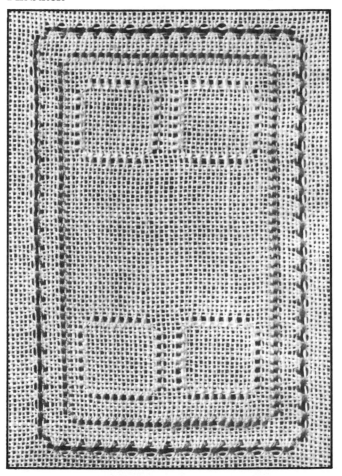

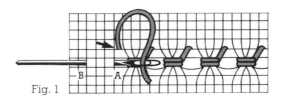

Fig. 1

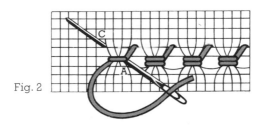

Fig. 2

This stitch is mainly used in Drawn Fabric embroidery either as a simple outline stitch as shown in the photograph or as a hem edge. It can also be used in Drawn Thread embroidery and for outlining appliqué work. Fig. 1 – bring the thread out at the arrow, insert the needle at A (2 threads down, or the required number) and bring out at B (4 threads to the left), insert again at A and bring out again at B. Fig. 2 – insert the needle again at A and bring out at C (2 threads up and 4 threads to the left). Continue in this way for the required length. All stitches must be pulled firmly. The working method is basically the same for the other types of embroidery mentioned. For a hem edge or appliqué, the stitches would be worked through the extra double thickness of fabric to anchor the edges.

Drawn Thread Stitches
Hemstitch

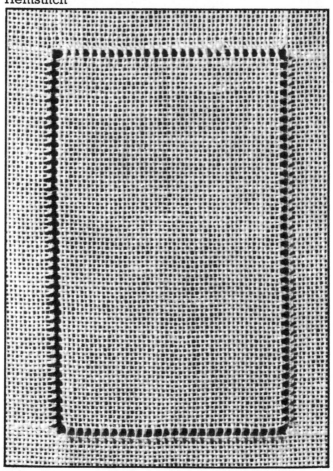

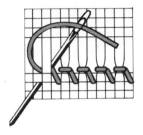

Measure the required depth of hem plus the turnings and withdraw the required number of threads. Do not withdraw the threads right across the fabric, but only to form a square or rectangle. Cut the threads at the centre and withdraw gradually outwards on each side to within the hem measurement, leaving a sufficient length of thread at the corners to darn the ends invisibly. Turn back the hem to the space of the drawn threads, mitre corners and baste. Bring the working thread out 2 threads down (or the required number) from the space of drawn threads through the folded hem at right hand side, pass the needle behind and round 2 loose vertical threads, bringing the needle out 2 threads down through all the folds of the hem in readiness for the next stitch.

Ladder Hemstitch

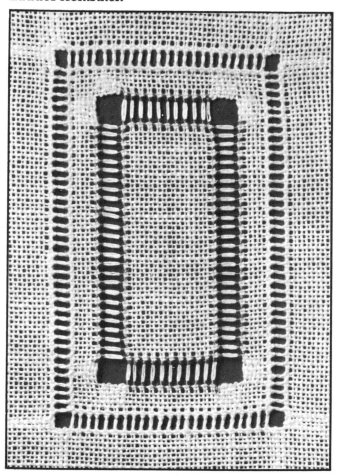

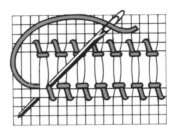

This stitch is worked in the same way as Hemstitch, with the Hemstitch being worked along both edges of the space of drawn threads and may be worked on any weight of even-weave fabric.

Interlaced Hemstitch

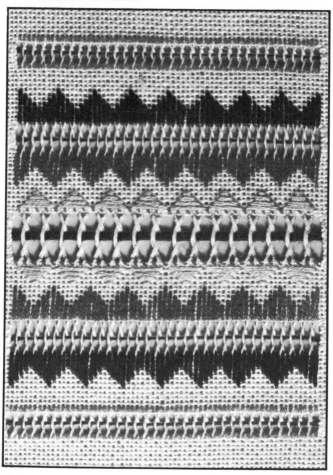

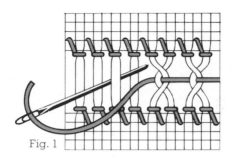

Fig. 1

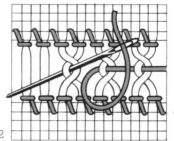

Fig. 2

Work Ladder Hemstitch first for the length required. Fasten a long thread centrally at the right hand side of the loose threads. Fig. 1 – pass the working thread across the front of two groups of threads and insert the needle from left to right under the second group. Fig. 2 – twist the second group over the first group by inserting the needle under the first group from right to left. Pull the thread through. The interlaced thread should be pulled firmly to lie in position through the centre of the twisted groups.

Zig-Zag Hemstitch

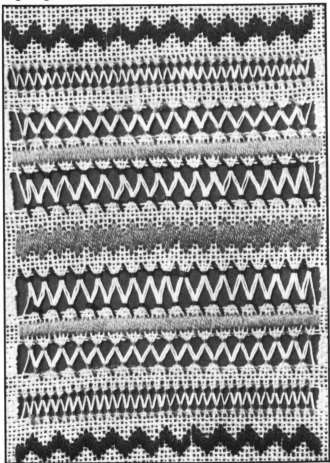

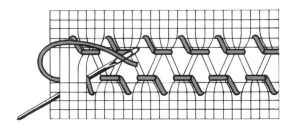

This variation is worked in the same way as Hemstitch, but there must be an even number of threads in each group of loose threads caught together in the first row. In the second row, the groups are divided in half, so that each group is composed of half the number of threads from one group and half from the adjacent group. A half group starts and ends the second row.

Italian or Double Hemstitch

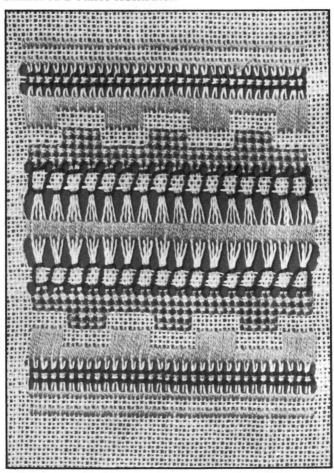

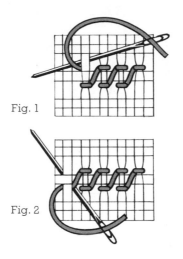

Fig. 1

Fig. 2

Withdraw threads from the fabric for the required width, miss the required number of threads and withdraw another band of the same number of threads. Fig. 1 – bring the thread out 2 loose threads to the left (or the required number) in the upper band of drawn threads; pass the needle around and behind the 2 loose threads and bring out where the thread first emerged. Fig. 2 – pass the thread down vertically over 2 fabric threads and pass the needle behind and around the 2 loose threads to the left on the lower band of drawn threads, pass the needle diagonally behind the fabric emerging 2 threads up and 2 threads to the left in the upper band of drawn threads in readiness for the next stitch. These two movements are worked throughout.

Diamond Hemstitch

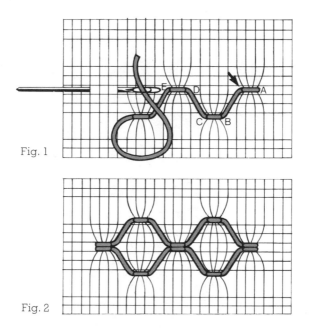

Fig. 1

Fig. 2

Withdraw threads from the fabric for the required width, miss
the required number of threads and withdraw another band
of the same number of threads. Fig. 1 – bring the thread out at
the arrow. Insert the needle at A (4 threads to the right, or the
required number) and bring out again at the arrow, insert at B
(3 threads down) pass the needle behind 4 loose threads and
bring out at C, insert again at B, and bring out at C, insert the
needle at D (3 threads up) and bring out at E (4 threads to the
left), insert again at D and bring out at E. Continue in this way
to the end of the row. Fig. 2 – turn the fabric round and work
the second row in the same way with the connecting stitches
of the second row worked into the same holes as the stitches
of the first row.

Reversed Wave Stitch

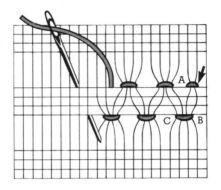

Withdraw threads from the fabric for the required width, miss the required number of threads and withdraw another band of the same number of threads. Bring the thread out at the arrow. Pass the needle over 2 loose threads to the left (or the required number) in the upper band of drawn threads and insert at A, bring out at B (4 threads down and 2 threads to the right), insert at C (4 loose threads to the left) and bring out at A (4 threads up and 2 threads to the right). Continue in this way to the end of the row, finishing the upper edge with a stitch over 2 loose threads to balance with the beginning.

Open Lacing Stitch

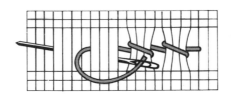

Fasten a long thread centrally at the right hand side of the loose threads. Insert the needle under 4 loose threads (or the required number) and take a backward stitch over and around the same 4 threads and bring the needle out 8 threads to the left in readiness for the next stitch. Continue in this way to the end of the row.

Needleweaving

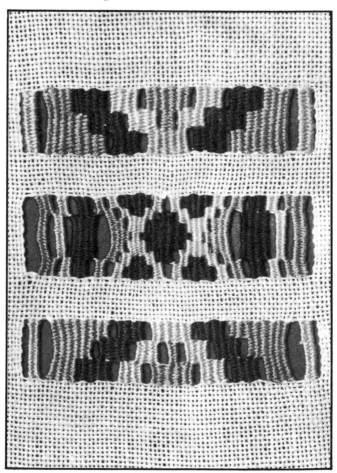

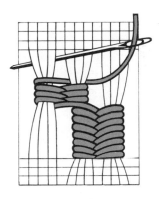

Withdraw threads from the fabric for the required width of the needleweaving pattern. When working with a fairly heavy fabric and using thick embroidery thread, one row of weaving (back and forward) is usually sufficient to replace one drawn thread of fabric. The pattern consists of blocks of weaving with an even number of stitches in each block. Generally the blocks are worked diagonally across the loose threads using different shades interconnecting to form attractive patterns, as seen in the photograph. The diagram gives the basic working method for all Needleweaving showing the connecting stitch worked over and under the loose threads common to both blocks, thus forming the link between each block.

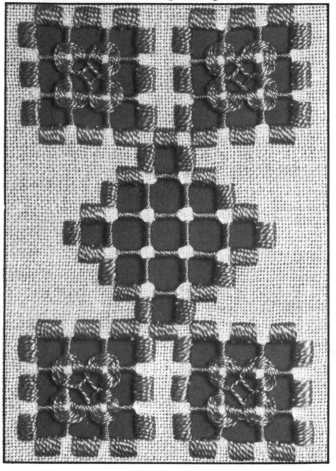

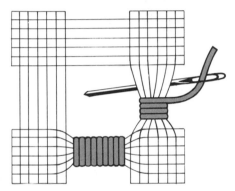

Fig. 1

To work the Overcast Bars, withdraw the number of threads required from the fabric and separate the loose threads into bars by overcasting firmly over these threads as many times as required to cover the groups of threads completely, as shown in fig. 1.

(continued overleaf)

Overcast Bars and Darning Filling Stitch
(continued)

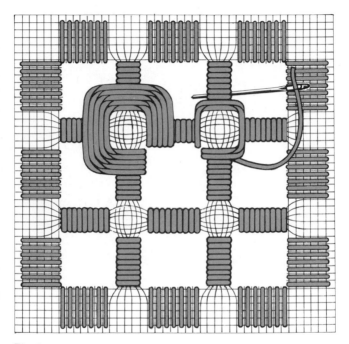

Fig. 2

Darning Filling Stitch is worked at the intersections of the bars by passing the needle over and under the bars from right to left then left to right over the corners of the outer squares leaving the corner of the inner square empty as shown in fig. 2.

Fig. 3

On completion of the four corners work a Dove's Eye Filling Stitch in the inner square as shown in fig. 3.

Woven Bars

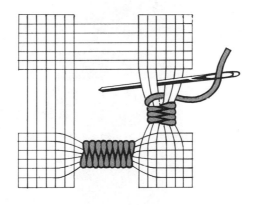

To work Woven Bars, withdraw an even number of threads from the fabric and separate the loose threads into bars by weaving over and under an even number of threads until the threads are completely covered.

Woven Bars with Picots in Post Stitch

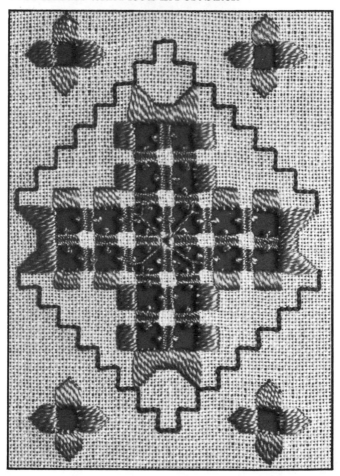

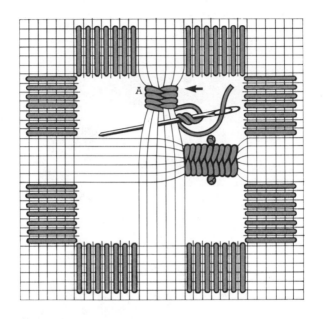

Bring the thread out at the arrow, insert 3 threads to the left
and bring out at A, insert 3 threads to the right. Continue in
this way until there are four woven stitches (8 stitches) in all.
To form the Post Stitch on the fifth bar (9th stitch) twist the
thread twice round the needle in a clockwise direction and
insert as shown in the diagram, hold the twisted threads firmly
in position with left thumb while still on the needle and push
needle through to form a knot. Turn fabric so that completed
knot is to left hand side, work a second knot in the same way,
this time previous knot and twisted thread on needle are both
held firmly in position beneath left thumb, pull the needle
through to form knot. Complete by working four more woven
stitches (8 stitches).

Twisted Bars and Branch Filling Stitch

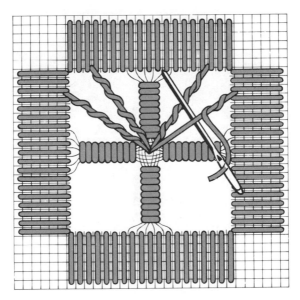

Fig. 1

To work Twisted Bars carry the thread diagonally across the space entering the fabric as shown, twisting the thread over the first thread as required back to the starting point. Twisted Bars may also be worked singly across a space, the thread emerging centrally at a corner between one vertical and one horizontal set of Satin Stitch blocks. The method of forming the bar is the same.

(continued overleaf)

Twisted Bars and Branch Filling Stitch (continued)

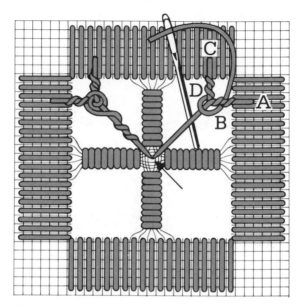

Fig. 2

To work Branch Filling Stitch, bring the thread out in the centre at arrow. Insert the needle at A (3 fabric threads to the right) and bring out at B and twist twice. Insert at C (3 fabric threads up) and bring out at D and twist twice. Pass the thread over the diagonal thread and pass under right hand branch and over left hand branch then pass the thread under the diagonal thread as shown in diagram. Pass over and under once more to complete knot. Twist thread round diagonal thread required number of times and bring out at centre in readiness to start once more.

Festoon Filling Stitch. Working diagram on following page

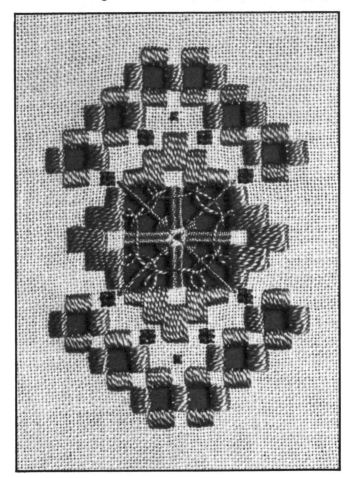

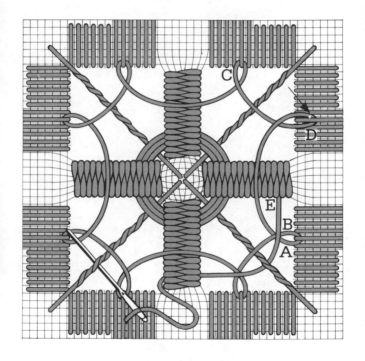

Work the Woven, Twisted Bars and Darned Wheel then bring the thread out at the arrow (7 Satin Stitches down and 3 fabric threads to the right). Pass the thread over a Woven Bar and round the fifth Satin Stitch down (inserting at A and emerging at B), continue in this way until the thread emerges at C, pass the thread over the Twisted Bar and insert at D (8 Satin Stitches down and 3 fabric threads to the right) emerging on the wrong side, conceal the working thread behind the 4 remaining Satin Stitches and for a few stitches behind the Woven Bar and bring out at E, still on the wrong side, pass the thread over the twisted loop and under the Twisted Bar. Continue in this way to complete the filling. Finish off by inserting the needle on the wrong side of the Woven Bar at E and passing the thread behind a few stitches neatly.

Ribbed Wheel Filling Stitch

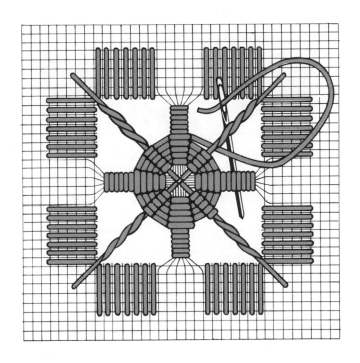

Work the Overcast Bars, then work the four Twisted Bars diagonally across the spaces. The centre is formed by taking a Back Stitch over each Overcast and Twisted Bar, continue in this way until the wheel reaches the desired size.

Darned Wheel Filling Stitch

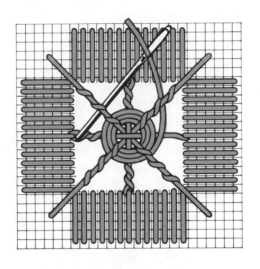

Work four Twisted Bars across the space two diagonally, one
vertically and one horizontally. On the fourth bar twist the
thread to the centre only then commence darning by passing
the needle under and over the spokes formed by the bars,
continue in this way until the wheel reaches the desired size.
To finish, complete the twisting of the fourth bar.

Spider's Web Filling Stitch

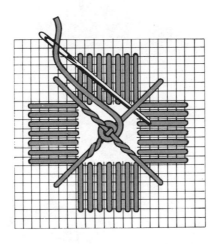

Two Twisted Bars are worked across the space, but the twisting of the second bar is taken to the centre only. The thread is then darned under and over the spokes formed by the bars two or three times in the centre. To finish, complete the twisting of the second bar.

Oblique Loop Filling Stitch

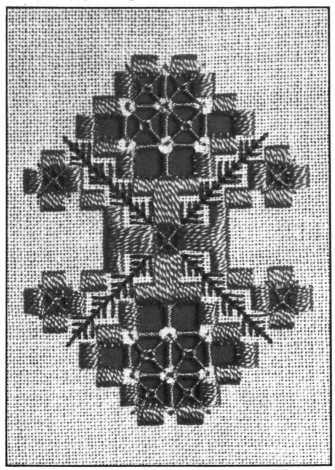

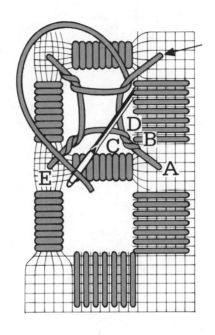

Work the Overcast Bars, then bring the thread out at the arrow, insert the needle at A and bring out at B, pass the needle under the thread at C and bring out at D, insert the needle at E and continue in this way to complete.

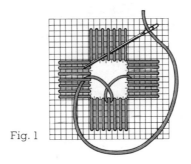

Fig. 1

Fig. 1 – shows the method of working Dove's Eye Filling Stitch
which is composed of four looped stitches one on each side of
space left by the cut fabric threads. The stitches are taken
under the central stitch with the thread under the needle. To
complete the last loop, pass the needle under the commencing
stitch and insert into the fabric at the other side of the central
stitch. This stitch may be worked between Woven Bars,
Overcast Bars, blocks and bars or loose threads. The stitches
are worked into the centre of Woven Bars, but worked completely over the Overcast Bars and loose threads.

(continued overleaf)

Dove's Eye and Lace Filling Stitches (continued)

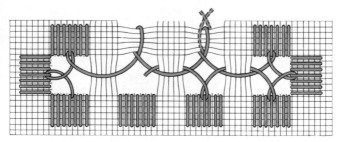

Fig. 2

Fig. 2 – shows the method of working Lace Filling Stitch (over a row of spaces flanked by loose threads. Commence at the left hand side over a space between blocks and work along the top line making (Buttonhole Stitch) loops over the groups of loose threads. Complete the right hand corner space, then work along the lower line, passing the needle over the loops made by the first row and behind the groups of loose threads. Where rows of Lace.Filling Stitch occur over rows of spaces flanked on the four sides by loose threads, the second and following rows are worked in the same way, but with the lower loop of the stitch over the same group of loose threads as the upper loop of the previous row (see dotted line).

Alphabetical Index

Alphabetical Index

B	Page
Back Stitch	10
Back Stitch, Ringed	40
Back Stitch, Whipped	10
Bars, Overcast	92
Bars, Twisted	100
Bars, Woven	96
Bars, Woven with Post Stitch Picots	98
Branch Filling Stitch	100

C	
Cable Stitch	36
Chevron Stitch	22
Coil Filling Stitch	54
Cretan Stitch	24
Cross Stitch	14
Cross Stitch, Double	16

D	
Darned Wheel Filling Stitch	108
Darning Filling Stitch	92
Diagonal Raised Band	62
Diamond Hemstitch	84
Double Cross Stitch	16
Double Faggot Filling Stitch	58
Double Hemstitch	82
Double Running Stitch	12
Dove's Eye Filling Stitch	114

E	
Edging Stitch, Pointed	69
Edging Stitch, Squared	66
Eyelet Hole	38

F	
Faggot Filling Stitch, Double	58
Faggot Filling Stitch, Reversed	60
Fern Stitch	28
Festoon Filling Stitch	103
Filling Stitch, Branch	100
Filling Stitch, Coil	54
Filling Stitch, Darned Wheel	108
Filling Stitch, Darning	92
Filling Stitch, Double Faggot	58

Filling Stitch, Dove's Eye   114
Filling Stitch, Festoon   103
Filling Stitch, Honeycomb   50
Filling Stitch, Lace   114
Filling Stitch, Linked Four-sided   56
Filling Stitch, Mosaic   64
Filling Stitch, Oblique Loop   112
Filling Stitch, Reversed Faggot   60
Filling Stitch, Ribbed Wheel   106
Filling Stitch, Spider's Web   110
Florentine Stitch   34
Fly Stitch   26
Four-sided Stitch and Filling   42
Four-sided Filling Stitch, Linked   56
Four-sided Wave Stitch   48

H
Hemstitch   74
Hemstitch, Diamond   84
Hemstitch, Double   82
Hemstitch, Interlaced   78
Hemstitch, Italian   82
Hemstitch, Ladder   76
Hemstitch, Zig-Zag   80
Herringbone Stitch   20
Holbein Stitch   12
Hole, Eyelet   38
Honeycomb Filling Stitch   50

I
Interlaced Hemstitch   78
Italian Hemstitch   82

L
Lace Filling Stitch   114
Lacing Stitch, Open   88
Ladder Hemstitch   76
Linked Four-sided Filling Stitch   56
Loop Filling Stitch, Oblique   112

M
Mosaic Filling Stitch   64

N
Needleweaving   90

O

Oblique Loop Filling Stitch 112
Open Lacing Stitch 88
Overcast Bars 92

P

Pin Stitch 72
Pointed Edging Stitch 69
Punch Stitch 52

R

Raised Band, Diagonal 62
Reversed Faggot Filling Stitch 60
Reversed Wave Stitch 86
Ribbed Wheel Filling Stitch 106
Rice Stitch 18
Ringed Back Stitch 40
Running Stitch, Double 12

S

Satin Stitch 32
Spider's Web Filling Stitch 110
Squared Edging Stitch 66
Star Stitch 30

T

Three-sided Stitch 44
Twisted Bars 100

W

Wave Stitch and Filling 46
Wave Stitch, Four-sided 48
Wave Stitch, Reversed 86
Wheel Filling Stitch, Darned 108
Wheel Filling Stitch, Ribbed 106
Whipped Back Stitch 10
Woven Bars 96
Woven Bars with Picots in Post Stitch 98

Z

Zig-Zag Hemstitch 80